# Ceratophrys: Horned Frogs as Pets
## Common name "Pac Man Frogs"

Argentine Horned Frog, Ornate Horned and South American Horned Frog Care

Breeding, habitat, health, food, diet, lifespan, care sheet and diseases facts.

By Taylor David

**Ceratophrys:**
**Horned Frogs as Pets**
**Common name "Pac Man Frogs"**

Author: Taylor David
ISBN 978-1-927870-43-3

Copyright © 2013 Ubiquitous Publishing
ubiquitouspublishing.com
Published in Canada

Printed in the USA

All rights reserved. No part of this book may be reproduced or transmitted in any form or by any means, electronic or mechanical, including photocopying, recording or by any information storage and retrieval system, without written permission from the author, except for the inclusion of brief quotations in a review.

# Ceratophrys:
## Horned Frogs as Pets

## Common name "Pac Man Frogs"

Argentine Horned Frog, Ornate Horned and South American Horned Frog Care

Includes Pac Man Frog care, breeding, habitat, health, food, diet, lifespan, care sheet and diseases facts.

# Foreword

Although the title of the book is " Ceratophrys: Horned Frogs as Pets," the more common name in the pet community to refer to these frogs is "Pac Man Frogs." For this reason, these horned frogs will be referred to as such throughout this book since it's the term readers are most familiar with and most used. (Disclaimer: Please note that this is in no way affiliated with the "Pac Man" video game by Namco Bandai Games Inc. Rather, the term is used in a completely different context with a different meaning).

In this book you will find all of the information you need to be prepared for becoming a Pac Man Frog owner. You will find information about Pac Man Frog care, care sheet, cages, enclosure, habitat, diet, facts, set up, food, names, pictures, info, life span, breeding, feeding and cost. After reading this book, you will be an expert on Pac Man Frogs!

## Acknowledgements

I would like to extend my sincerest thanks to my loving spouse. Thank you for always encouraging me to pursue my passions, no matter how strange they may be. Additional thanks to my editor for a lot of help putting this together.

# Table of Contents

Chapter One: Introduction ............................................................. 1

Chapter Two: Understanding Pac Man Frogs ..................... 3

    1.) What Are Pac Man Frogs? ................................................. 3

    2.) Facts about Pac Man Frogs ............................................... 6

        Summary of Facts ................................................................ 8

    3.) Conservation Status of Horned Frogs ........................... 9

    4.) Types of Horned Frogs ..................................................... 11

    5.) Life Stages of the Horned Frog ...................................... 19

Chapter Three: What to Know Before You Buy ................. 21

    1.) Do You Need a License? .................................................. 21

        a.) Licensing in the U.S. ..................................................... 22

        b.) Licensing in the U.K. .................................................... 22

    2.) How Many Should You Buy? ........................................... 24

    3.) Can Pac Man Frogs Be Kept with Other Pets? ............ 25

    4.) Ease and Cost of Care ...................................................... 26

        a.) Initial Costs ..................................................................... 26

        b.) Monthly Costs ................................................................ 29

    5.) Pros and Cons of Pac Man Frogs .................................... 31

Chapter Four: Purchasing Pac Man Frogs ........................... 33

    1.) Where to Buy Pac Man Frogs .......................................... 33

a.) Buying in the U.S. ..................................................34

b.) Buying in the U.K. ..................................................34

2.) How to Select a Healthy Pac Man Frog ....................36

# Chapter Five: Caring for Pac Man Frogs ..........................39

1.) Habitat Requirements ................................................40

a.) Choosing a Substrate ...........................................40

b.) Heating and Lighting ..........................................41

c.) Additional Features .............................................42

d.) Summary of Habitat Info ....................................43

2.) Feeding Pac Man Frogs ..............................................44

a.) Nutritional Needs ................................................44

b.) How Much to Feed .............................................45

c.) Types of Food ......................................................47

d.) Feeding Info Summary .......................................49

3.) Breeding Pac Man Frogs .............................................50

a.) Basic Breeding Info ..............................................50

b.) The Breeding Process ..........................................51

c.) Raising the Tadpoles ............................................53

d.) Breeding Info Summary: .....................................55

# Chapter Six: Keeping Your Frogs Healthy ........................57

1.) Common Health Problems ........................................57

2.) Preventing Illness .......................................................71

Chapter Seven: Pac Man Frogs Care Sheet ............................ 73

    1.) Basic Information ........................................................ 73

    2.) Cage Set-up Summary ................................................ 74

    3.) Feeding Info Summary ............................................... 74

    4.) Breeding Info Summary .............................................. 75

Chapter Eight: Common Mistakes Owners Make ................ 77

Chapter Nine: Frequently Asked Questions ........................ 83

    1.) General Questions ....................................................... 83

    2.) Questions about Feeding ........................................... 87

    3.) Tank Setup and Maintenance Questions ................... 89

    4.) Horned Frog Care Questions ..................................... 93

    5.) Questions about Breeding .......................................... 95

Chapter Ten: Relevant Websites .......................................... 97

    1.) Food for Pac Man Frogs ............................................. 97

    2.) Care for Pac Man Frogs ............................................. 99

    3.) Health Info for Pac Man Frogs ................................ 101

    4.) General Info for Pac Man Frogs .............................. 102

Index .................................................................................... 104

References ........................................................................... 109

Photo Credits ...................................................................... 114

## Chapter One: Introduction

If you are looking for a unique pet for you and your family, look no further than the Pac Man Frog. These frogs are very large and exhibit an array of interesting color patterns. One of the most exciting things about these frogs is watching them eat – these frogs are voracious eaters, eager to consume crickets, worms and even pinkie mice!

Once you set up your frog's tank, these animals are not very difficult to keep. You will need to clean out the tank once in a while and provide a healthy, varied diet, but other than that these frogs have few needs. These frogs live an average

## Chapter One: Introduction

of 6 to 10 years in captivity so you will be able to enjoy your frog for years to come!

If you would like to learn more about these fascinating creatures, keep reading! In this book you will find all of the information you need to know about buying horned frogs, setting up their tank and feeding them a proper diet. You will also receive valuable information about common health problems, frequently asked questions and even breeding tips. What are you waiting for? Get started!

## Chapter Two: Understanding Pac Man Frogs

### 1.) What Are Pac Man Frogs?

The name horned frog applies to a genus of frogs called *Ceratophrys* in the family Leptodactylidae. These frogs also go by the name Pac Man Frogs because of their wide mouths and stomachs. The two most popular species of horned frog are *Ceratophrys ornata* and *Ceratophrys cranwelli*, or the ornate horned frog and the Cranwell's horned frog, respectively.

## Chapter Two: Understanding Pac Man Frogs

The ornate horned frog is known by many names, the most common of which are the Pac Man Frog or the Argentine Horned Frog. The name "horned frog" was given in reference to the pointed upper lids over the eyes of these frogs which resemble horns. These frogs are naturally found throughout Argentina, Paraguay, Uruguay and Brazil – they tend to burrow into the damp, leafy vegetation of the rainforest floor.

These frogs tend to grow very large, up to 6 inches (15 cm) long and they can be quite aggressive. Most of their time, however, is spent burrowed into the ground. Pac Man Frogs are generally green with black or red markings, though their coloring may vary according to region. When these frogs feel threatened, they will puff up to make themselves appear larger and emit a loud, scream-like sound.

Pac Man Frogs are fairly inactive. Most of their time is spent burrowed into the substrate of the rainforest floor and, when they emerge to eat, they typically sit in wait for food to come to them. These frogs prey on large insects, rodents, lizards, small birds and even other frogs. If properly fed and cared for, these frogs can live up to 10 years in captivity, though the average lifespan is closer to 6 or 7 years.

## Chapter Two: Understanding Pac Man Frogs

# Did You Know...

- Horned frogs are sometimes called "mouths with legs" because their mouths take up such a large portion of their bodies

- Though adult horned frogs are inactive feeders, juveniles are cannibalistic and highly active feeders

- Horned frogs have teeth on the roof of their mouths as well as around the outside of the jaw

- All frogs, including the horned frog, sleep with their eyes open

- Horned frogs have very sensitive skin – their skin acts as a supplemental breathing organ and the oil from human skin can be damaging to horned frogs

- Frogs can be differentiated from toads by their smooth skin – toads have textured skin

## Chapter Two: Understanding Pac Man Frogs

### 2.) Facts about Pac Man Frogs

Pac Man Frogs are large and fat – most of their body seems to be taken up by their giant mouths. These frogs are typically green or yellowish green in color with dark red or black markings along the back. The average size of these frogs is about 5.5 inches (14 cm), though they can grow up to 6 inches (15 cm) in length.

Unlike many breeds, the female Pac Man Frog is typically larger than the male. Females can reach a weight of up to 1 lbs. (480 g). Aside from their size, there are a few other

## Chapter Two: Understanding Pac Man Frogs

ways to differentiate between male and female frogs. Male horned frogs tend to croak more often than females and they often exhibit spotting on the chest. Male horned frogs may also have spots on their pads while females do not.

In captivity, Pac Man Frogs generally live 6 to 7 years on average but they can live as long as 10 years. These frogs do best in an aquarium or terrarium outfitted with moist, loose substrate and a shallow bowl of water. The temperature in the tank should be kept stable between 75° and 80° F (24° to 27° C) during the day and it may be allowed to drop a few degrees at night. These frogs can be fed a variety of insects and worms as well as the occasional fish or mouse.

Because these frogs have very fragile skin, it is best to keep handling to a minimum. Human skin contains oils which can be damaging to the skin of horned frogs. Additionally, Pac Man Frogs have small, sharp teeth that can inflict a great deal of pain if they bite you. If you are not looking for a pet that you can handle on a regular basis, the Pac Man Frog may be a good option for you and your family.

# Chapter Two: Understanding Pac Man Frogs

## *Summary of Facts*

**Scientific Name**: *Ceratophrys ornata*
**Other Names**: Ornate Horned Frog, Argentine Horned Frog, South American Horned Frog
**Size**: up to 6 inches (15 cm)
**Weight**: up to 1 lbs. (480 g)
**Color**: green or yellowish green with black or red markings on the back
**Diet**: crickets, worms, feeder fish, snails, mice
**Lifespan**: 6 to 7 years average, up to 10 in captivity

## Chapter Two: Understanding Pac Man Frogs

### 3.) Conservation Status of Horned Frogs

The various species of horned frog were once abundant throughout South America but in recent years, their numbers have dwindled to dangerously low levels. Several species including the Venezuelan, Caatinga and Pacific Horned Frog have already been given "vulnerable" or "near threatened" status by the International Union for Conservation of Nature and Natural Resources (IUCN). Even the Pac Man Frog has been labeled "near threatened".

According to the IUCN Red List entry published in 2004, the Pac Man Frog population is in significant decline. It has not yet been labeled "vulnerable," however, because the population is declining at a rate of less than 30% over ten years. It has been noted that this species has disappeared from at least two different sites in Uruguay and it has become rare in Argentina. The major threat to horned frogs is habitat loss.

**Population decline may be due to several factors including:**

- Agricultural and housing development
- Water and soil pollution (due to agriculture and industry)
- Over-collection for the international pet trade

## Chapter Two: Understanding Pac Man Frogs

- Collection of eggs sold for scientific research
- Persecution due to unfounded beliefs that these frogs are venomous

Before you purchase a horned frog, make sure that it was captive bred and not wild-caught. Do your part to help preserve this beautiful species in the wild.

## Chapter Two: Understanding Pac Man Frogs

### 4.) Types of Horned Frogs

Horned frogs belong to the genus Ceratophrys in the family Leptodactylidae. This genus contains eight different species of horned frogs:

- *Ceratophrys aurita*
- *Ceratophrys calcarata*
- *Ceratophrys cornuta* – Surinam Horned Frog
- *Ceratophrys cranwelli* – Cranwell's Horned Frog
- *Ceratophrys joazeirensis*
- *Ceratophrys ornata* – Pac Man Frog
- *Ceratophrys stolzmanni*
- *Ceratophrys testudo*

## Chapter Two: Understanding Pac Man Frogs

**Ceratophrys aurita**

This species is also known by the name Brazilian Horned Frog. These frogs are endemic to Brazil where they inhabit the tropical and subtropical lowland forests and freshwater marshes. This species is not commonly kept as a pet and its numbers in the wild are dwindling due to habitat loss.

**Natural Habitat**: Brazil; found in tropical and subtropical lowland forests and freshwater marshes

## Chapter Two: Understanding Pac Man Frogs

*Ceratophrys calcarata*

This frog is often called the Venezuelan Horned Frog, or the Sapo Cuaima. This species is found in both Venezuela and Colombia in the dry savannah as well as tropical and subtropical shrubland and grassland – they can also be found in freshwater marshes. This species is also threatened by habitat loss.

**Natural Habitat**: Venezuela and Colombia; found in dry savannah as well as tropical and subtropical shrub land, grassland and freshwater marshes

Chapter Two: Understanding Pac Man Frogs

## Ceratophrys cornuta – Surinam Horned Frog

The Surinam Horned Frog is also known as the Amazonian Horned Frog. This species is found in the northern parts of South America and it grows up to 7.5 inches (20 cm) in the wild. This species was once thought to be the same species as the Pac Man Frog but it was eventually discovered that, because it lives in a different habitat and does not interbreed with the Pac Man Frog in the wild, it was a different species.

**Natural Habitat:** northern part of South America

## Chapter Two: Understanding Pac Man Frogs

### *Ceratophrys joazeirensis*

This species is also known as the Caatinga Horned Frog and it is endemic to Brazil. These frogs can generally be found throughout the dry savannah as well as in tropical or subtropical shrubland and grassland. Like several species of horned frog, this species' habitat is threatened.

**Natural Habitat**: Brazil; found throughout the dry savannah as well as in tropical or subtropical shrub land and grassland

## Chapter Two: Understanding Pac Man Frogs

### *Ceratophrys cranwelli* – Cranwell's Horned Frog

Cranwell's Horned Frogs are one of the more popular horned frog species to be kept as pets. These frogs are endemic to the Gran Chaco region of Argentina where they spend most of their time burrowed into the ground, waiting for prey to approach. This species grows up to 5 inches (13 cm) long and can weigh up to 1 lbs. (0.5 kg). Cranwell's Horned Frogs are typically dark green or brown in color but they can also be found in albino variants, exhibiting yellow and orange coloration.

**Natural Habitat**: endemic to the Gran Chaco region of Argentina

## Chapter Two: Understanding Pac Man Frogs

### *Ceratophrys stolzmanni*

Also known as the Pacific Horned Frog, this species is typically found throughout Ecuador and Peru. The Pacific Horned Frog lives in tropical or subtropical dry forests, shrubland and sandy shores. This species is sometimes kept as a pet and its conservation status is "Vulnerable" due to habitat loss.

**Natural Habitat:** Ecuador and Peru; found in tropical or subtropical dry forests, shrub land and sandy shores

## Chapter Two: Understanding Pac Man Frogs

***Ceratophrys testudo***

This species is endemic to Ecuador which is why it is also known as the Ecuadorian Horned Frog. These frogs live in tropical or subtropical montane forests as well as in intermittent freshwater marshes.

**Natural Habitat**: Ecuador; found in tropical or subtropical montane forests and intermittent freshwater marshes

# Chapter Two: Understanding Pac Man Frogs

## 5.) Life Stages of the Horned Frog

### Eggs and Tadpoles

A female Pac Man Frog can lay between 1,000 and 2,000 eggs at a time. Females generally lay their eggs on broad-leafed plants so it is a good idea to furnish your breeding tank with a variety of foliage. Once spawned, the eggs take 2 to 4 days to hatch into tadpoles.

Horned frog tadpoles have rounded bodies with a long tail and no legs. The process of metamorphosis is the process by which tadpoles transform into juvenile frogs – this process generally takes between 3 and 5 weeks. These tadpoles tend to be carnivorous, so if you want to raise many of them to maturity, you should separate them into individual cups.

### Juvenile Frogs

As the tadpoles metamorphose, they begin to develop four legs starting with the back legs and ending with the front legs. The frog's eyes will begin to bulge out from its body and the tail will slowly be absorbed. Over time, the frog's mouth widens and its lungs begin to develop.

Once the lungs are fully developed, the juvenile frog can live on land. In order for juvenile frogs to grow properly

# Chapter Two: Understanding Pac Man Frogs

into mature adults, they must be fed on a daily basis. Young crickets are the ideal food for juvenile frogs because they contain a variety of nutrients and are small enough for juvenile frogs to catch and eat.

## **Adult Frogs**

It can take as long as 2 or 3 years for Pac Man Frogs to reach full maturity. In adulthood, these frogs can measure up to 6 inches (15 cm) in length and may weigh as much as 1 lbs. (0.45 kg). Adult horned frogs have very wide mouths and a voracious appetite – they are capable of eating much larger prey than many frog species. This species thrives on crickets, large worms, snails and even small birds. In captivity, the diets of these frogs can be supplemented with pinkie mice and feeder fish.

## Chapter Three: What to Know Before You Buy

### 1.) Do You Need a License?

Whether or not you are required to obtain a permit or license to keep Pac Man Frogs depends on where you live. Before you purchase a horned frog, take the time to determine the licensing regulations in your area. It is always better to be safe than sorry.

## Chapter Three: What to Know Before you Buy

*a.) Licensing in the U.S.*

In the United States, the Fish and Wildlife Service is responsible for regulating the capture, possession and sale of wild animals. Generally, only species that are native to the U.S. or listed as an endangered species are affected by federal law. There may, however, be individual state laws regulating the sale and keeping of non-native wildlife such as the horned frog.

In many cases, Pac Man Frog owners are not required to have a special permit or license. If you plan to breed or sell your frogs, however, the licensing requirements may be different. To determine whether your state has any regulations regarding keeping non-native amphibians, check with your local council. If a permit is required, it is generally fairly easy to obtain and fill out an application. In most cases, application fees are $50 (£38) or less.

*b.) Licensing in the U.K.*

In the United Kingdom, the Dangerous Wild Animals Act of 1976 prohibits individuals from keeping species of reptile and amphibian that are considered dangerous. These species may include alligators, caimans, asps and crocodiles. Pac Man Frogs are generally not considered

## Chapter Three: What to Know Before you Buy

dangerous and they have not been officially classified as endangered, so you most likely do not need to obtain a permit to keep one of these frogs in the U.K. To be absolutely sure, however, you should contact your local council.

**Remember, licensing requirements may be different for captive-bred and wild-caught specimens. In many areas of the U.S., the importation of non-native wildlife is restricted or regulated. Be sure to go through all of the appropriate legal channels in purchasing your horned frogs.

## Chapter Three: What to Know Before you Buy

### 2.) How Many Should You Buy?

Because horned frogs tend to be voracious eaters (and sometimes cannibalistic), they are best kept individually. If you try to keep a Pac Man Frog with other amphibians or reptiles, they may end up becoming prey for your frog. The only exception to this rule is in regard to breeding – if you plan to breed your frogs, one male and one female frog can be kept together. You should, however, keep an eye on the frogs to be sure they do not hurt each other.

## Chapter Three: What to Know Before you Buy

### 3.) Can Pac Man Frogs Be Kept with Other Pets?

For the same reasons mentioned earlier, Pac Man Frogs should not be kept in the same cage as other pets. As long as you keep your frog in its cage, however, there is no reason why they cannot be kept in the same household as cats, dogs and other household pets. Horned frogs are fairly inactive so they are not likely to attract the attention of other pets and, as long as you keep the cage out of reach, your pets are unlikely to bother your frog.

## Chapter Three: What to Know Before you Buy

### 4.) Ease and Cost of Care

Before you go out and buy a Pac Man Frog, you should be sure that you can handle both the initial and monthly costs of these pets. Not only do you have to think about the price of the frog itself but also of the tank and all of the necessary equipment. Once you cover those initial costs you must also think about the recurring monthly costs of keeping a pet horned frog.

### a.) Initial Costs

The initial costs for keeping a Pac Man Frog as a pet include the purchase price, tank, substrate, tank décor and heating/lighting.

**You will find a detailed explanation of these costs below:**

**Purchase Price**: The purchase price for a Pac Man Frog varies depending where you buy it. If you are able to find these frogs at your local pet store, they may cost you $25 to $40 (£19 - £30.50). If you buy your frog at a reptile expo, however, it may only cost you $10 to $20 (£7.50 - £15).

**Tank**: A basic 10-gallon glass aquarium is fairly inexpensive – you can probably find one at your local pet

## Chapter Three: What to Know Before you Buy

store for under $20 (£15). If you choose to keep your frog in a custom tank, or if you want a larger tank for a breeding pair, you could end up spending up to $100 (£76) on a tank for your frogs.

**Substrate**: Substrate is both an initial and a monthly cost for Pac Man Frogs. You will need enough substrate to set up your tank for the first time and then you will need to replace it occasionally as you clean out the tank. Substrate such as sphagnum moss generally costs less than $10 (£7.50).

**Tank Décor**: In addition to tank substrate, you also need to provide your horned frog with a water dish and places to hide. Your water dish may be something as simple as the kind of ceramic dish that collects water under potted plants – you may also use a plain plastic container. As far as hiding places go, you can make your own out of a terra cotta pot or some other material – you can also buy shelters made of bark or wood. The total cost for decorating your frog tank will most likely be between $10 and $30 (£7.50 - £23).

**Heating**: In order to create an authentic habitat for your frog you will need to keep the temperature stable. In order to do so, you should plan to purchase an under-tank heater – the kind made for reptiles. A small heater will cost you

## Chapter Three: What to Know Before you Buy

between $15 and $30 (£11.50 - £23). You may even be able to find a gently used heater online.

**Lighting:** The lighting needs of Pac Man Frogs are fairly basic – they simply need a fluorescent UVB lamp. If your tank has a screened lid you can buy a basic clip-on lamp and position it directly above your frog's water dish. The cost for a UVB lamp and bulb is generally between $15 and $20 (£11.50 - £15). You may already have an extra light fixture around your house that you can simply purchase a UVB bulb for.

**Summary of Initial Costs:**

| Initial Costs for Horned Frogs | | |
|---|---|---|
| Cost | One Frog | Breeding Pair |
| **Purchase Price** | $10 to $40 (£7.50 - £30.50) | $20 to $80 (£15 - £61) |
| **Tank/Terrarium** | $20 to $100 (£15 - £76) | $20 to $100 (£15 - £76) |
| **Substrate** | $10 (£7.50) | $10 (£7.50) |
| **Tank Décor** | $10 to $30 (£7.50 - £23) | $10 to $30 (£7.50 - £23) |

Chapter Three: What to Know Before you Buy

| | | |
|---|---|---|
| Lighting | $15 to $20 (£11.50 - £15) | $15 to $20 (£11.50 - £15) |
| Heating | $15 to $30 (£11.50 - £23) | $15 to $30 (£11.50 - £23) |
| Total: | $80 to $230 (£61 - £178) | $90 to $270 (£69 - £206) |

*b.) Monthly Costs*

The monthly costs for keeping a Pac Man Frog as a pet include the cost of food, substrate, supplements and other additional costs.

**You will find a detailed explanation of these costs below:**

**Food**: The most important recurring monthly cost for your horned frog is its food. Crickets are the main staple of most horned frogs and you can buy 250 of them (a three-month supply) for under $20 (£15). Additional foods such as worms, feeder fish and pinkie mice may add an extra $10 to $15 per month (£7.50 - £11.50), making the total monthly cost between $10 and $35 (£7.50 - £27).

**Supplements**: Vitamin and mineral supplements come in a variety of forms. You may choose to buy a single multi-

## Chapter Three: What to Know Before you Buy

vitamin formula or individual formulas for vitamins and minerals such as calcium and vitamin D3. A small container of powdered supplement should last you a month and will only cost about $5 (£3.80).

**Substrate:** As has already been mentioned, substrate is fairly inexpensive and you will only need to replace it when you clean your frog's tank. This being the case, you should only need to spend about $10 to $15 (£7.50 - £11.50) per month.

**Additional Costs:** Other costs you may want to factor into your budget include replacement bulbs, extra tank décor and a tank thermometer. The total cost for these items is not likely to be significant, probably under $15 (£11.50) per month.

**Summary of Monthly Costs:**

| \multicolumn{3}{c}{Initial Costs for Horned Frogs} |
|---|---|---|
| Cost | One Frog | Breeding Pair |
| Food | $10 to $35 (£7.50 - £27) | $20 to $70 (£15 - £53) |

## Chapter Three: What to Know Before you Buy

| | | |
|---|---|---|
| Supplements | $5 (£3.80) | $10 (£7.50) |
| Substrate | $10 to $15 (£7.50 - £11.50) | $10 to $15 (£7.50 - £11.50) |
| Additional Costs | $15 (£11.50) | $15 (£11.50) |
| Total: | $40 to $70 (£30 - £43) | $55 to $180 (£42 - £137) |

### 5.) Pros and Cons of Pac Man Frogs

Before you go out and purchase a Pac Man Frog, take the time to learn about the pros and cons of these frogs as pets. The more you know about these animals, the better prepared you will be to care for the properly.

**Pros for Horned Frogs**

- Despite their size, do not require a great deal of space to live
- Can be kept in a single cage – doesn't take up much room in the house
- Require little care other than stable heating/lighting and live food
- Unique appearance makes them interesting pets

## Chapter Three: What to Know Before you Buy

- Can be very interesting to watch them feed

**Cons for Horned Frogs**

- Require a varied diet of live prey
- Cannot be handled regularly because oils in human skin may cause harm
- May bite if handled improperly
- Over-collection is contributing to the decline of this species in the wild
- A permit or license may be required to keep them
- May spend most of their time buried in substrate (not visible)
- Some frogs may make a lot of noise

## Chapter Four: Purchasing Pac Man Frogs

### 1.) Where to Buy Pac Man Frogs

If you have determined that a Pac Man Frog really is the right pet for you, you may be ready to think about buying one. There are several ways to go about purchasing a frog, but some ways are better than others. Think carefully about where and how you purchase your horned frog so you are sure to get a healthy specimen.

# Chapter Four: Purchasing Pac Man Frogs

*a.) Buying in the U.S.*

In the United States, there are a few different options for buyingPac Man Frogs. You may, for example, be able to find them at your local pet store. If your store does not carry them, you may want to ask if they have contacts with a local supplier who may be willing to work with you. If not, you can always perform an online search for horned frog breeders.

Another option you may want to consider is attending a reptile and amphibian show. These shows are an excellent way to meet breeders and suppliers. You may get lucky and find someone at the show who is selling horned frogs, or you might be able to find someone who has a contact for you. Be wary of suppliers or online merchants who offer to ship the animal to you. During the shipping process, animals can be exposed to extreme temperatures and rough handling which could injure or even kill your frog.

*b.) Buying in the U.K.*

In the U.K., your options for buying a Pac Man Frog are the same as they are in the U.S. You can check your local pet store to see if they have horned frogs available or you can ask around for a recommendation of a supplier. Keep in

## Chapter Four: Purchasing Pac Man Frogs

mind, as you search for South American Dwarf Frogs, that it is preferable to buy frogs that are captive-bred rather than wild-caught.

Not only does purchasing captive-bred specimens mean that you are not supporting the trade that is destroying the natural habitat of horned frogs, but it may also be easier to keep captive-bred frogs. Frogs that have been taken from the wild may be more difficult to keep in captivity – they may not be as apt to accept food. Think carefully before purchasing a horned frog to ensure that the source you buy from is reputable.

## 2.) How to Select a Healthy Pac Man Frog

Observing Pac Man Frogs to ascertain their level of health is different from observing other types of frogs. Many species of frogs, for example, are very active so you can gauge their health by their level of activity. Pac Man Frogs, however, are very inactive so it is not necessarily a sign of ill health if the frog doesn't move very much.

Though you may not be able to ascertain a Pac Man Frog's health by its activity level, there are a few other things you can look for. Look for abnormal coloration, sores or damaged skin on the frog's body as these could be indications of disease. You should also be familiar enough

## Chapter Four: Purchasing Pac Man Frogs

with the overall appearance of the species to know whether everything is "normal" or not. The frog's eyes should be clear, not clouded or filmed over, and its nostrils should be clean and free of discharge. If possible, take the time to watch the frog eat – frogs that refuse food are often sick and can be very difficult to care for.

**Frogs are notoriously difficult to cure once they become ill. Save yourself the heartache of losing your horned frog by choosing a healthy one to begin with.

# Chapter Four: Purchasing Pac Man Frogs

## Chapter Five: Caring for Pac Man Frogs

Pac Man Frogs are not a difficult species to care for. As long as you provide them with a proper habitat and a healthy diet, you should have no trouble. In this chapter you will find all of the information you need to set up and maintain your frog's habitat – you will also learn how to create a healthy diet for your frog. Should you choose to breed your horned frog, you will also find information regarding breeding in this chapter.

## Chapter Five: Caring for Pac Man Frogs

### 1.) Habitat Requirements

Despite their large size, Pac Man Frogs do not require a very large terrarium – this is largely due to the fact that they are a fairly inactive species. The ideal tank size for horned frog is 10 gallons (38 liters). Even if you purchase your frog as a juvenile you should start out with a 10-gallon (38 liter) tank so you don't have to buy a new one when your frog grows. You can find a basic glass aquarium at your local pet store. If possible, find one that comes with a lid to prevent heat from escaping the tank.

Horned frogs are terrestrial frogs which means they live on land rather than in the water. They do, however, live in very moist natural environments so the tank should be kept damp and humid. In addition to moist substrate, you should also provide your frog with a shallow dish of water where it can soak. If your frog is still a juvenile, line the bottom of the dish with stones to raise the bottom.

#### *a.) Choosing a Substrate*

Sphagnum moss is the ideal substrate for a Pac Man Frog tank. It is soft so your frog can easily burrow into it and it will also retain moisture to keep your tank humid. If you don't want to line your entire tank with moss you can just

## Chapter Five: Caring for Pac Man Frogs

add clumps of it and line the tank with reptile carpet from your local pet store. You should also feel free to decorate the tank with live or artificial plants that will enhance the environment for your frog.

### b.) Heating and Lighting

Pac Man Frogs are naturally found in tropical and subtropical habitats. This being the case, their tank should be furnished to replicate this environment. Ideally, your frog's tank should be kept at a temperature between 75° and 80° F (24° to 27° C). To achieve this temperature, affix a

## Chapter Five: Caring for Pac Man Frogs

reptile heating pad to the underside of the tank and leave it on 24 hours a day.

In addition to this heating pad, set up a fluorescent light over the tank. This bulb should produce ultraviolet-B light. During the winter, you may need to replace this light with a red heat bulb to keep the temperature up. To monitor the temperature in your frog's tank, purchase an aquarium thermometer and affix it to the wall of the tank about 1 inch from the bottom. Make sure to place your frog's water dish in the warmest area of the tank.

### c.) Additional Features

In addition to heating and lighting your frog's tank, you also need to provide some shelter. In the wild, Pac Man Frogs spend a great deal of time hiding, burrowed into substrate. In their tank, it is important that your frogs have a place to hide. You can build a cave out of wide, flat rocks or provide a shelter made of bark. You can also arrange the tank so there is an overhang over the water dish where your frog can hide.

# Chapter Five: Caring for Pac Man Frogs

## d.) Summary of Habitat Info

**Ideal Tank Size**: 10 gallons (38 liters)
**Cage Type**: glass aquarium/terrarium
**Tank Temperature**: 75° and 80° F (24° to 27° C)
**Tank Environment**: damp and humid
**Heating**: reptile heating pad affixed to underside of the tank
**Lighting**: fluorescent UVB bulb; red heat bulb in winter
**Substrate**: soft and damp; sphagnum or peat moss
**Water**: shallow dish, cleaned daily
**Other**: hiding places, live or artificial plants

# Chapter Five: Caring for Pac Man Frogs

## 2.) Feeding Pac Man Frogs

The diet you offer your Pac Man Frogs will play a key role in its health and wellness. If your frog does not receive all of the nutrients it needs, it is unlikely to thrive. In this section you will learn everything you need to know about feeding your frog a healthy diet.

### *a.) Nutritional Needs*

Pac Man Frogs are carnivorous which means that the majority of their nutritional needs must be met by protein-based foods. In addition to protein, these frogs also require a certain balance of lipids (fats), vitamins and minerals. In order to create a healthy diet for your frog, you need to be aware of these nutritional needs.

Lipids are a very important part of your frog's diet, but you should be careful not to give too much. Too much fat in a frog's diet can lead to obesity. Ideally, your frog's need for lipids should be met by feeding insects – insects are generally between 10% and 30% fat and they also contain a number of vitamins and minerals.

Some of the most important vitamins and minerals for horned frogs to have in their diet include calcium,

## Chapter Five: Caring for Pac Man Frogs

phosphorus, vitamin A and vitamin D3. Captive frogs are especially at risk for vitamin A and vitamin D3 deficiency – these deficiencies can lead to serious health problems including metabolic bone disease.

*b.) How Much to Feed*

Pac Man Frogs are likely to eat any food you offer them. Because they are such voracious eaters, it can be easy to overfeed these frogs. Overfeeding, however, can result in obesity and a variety of other health problems so it is best

## Chapter Five: Caring for Pac Man Frogs

avoided. While your frog is still young, it may need to eat more frequently than a mature adult.

Small horned frogs should be offered 4 to 6 crickets on a daily basis. In case your frog doesn't eat all of the crickets at once, you should provide them with some oat bran to eat until your frog gets around to them. As your juvenile frog grows, you can cut back the feeding to three times a week. Once your frog is fully grown, you may only need to feed him once a week in large quantities. When your frog is large enough to accept them, you can begin adding small pinkie mice to its diet twice a month.

## Chapter Five: Caring for Pac Man Frogs

### c.) Types of Food

**Crickets**: Crickets are an easy, affordable source of food for horned frogs. If you ask at your local pet store, you should be able to get crickets of different sizes – young crickets for small frogs and adult crickets for mature frogs. It is easy to add mineral supplements to crickets – just sprinkle a little in the bag they came in and shake to coat. You should be aware that crickets can crawl into the substrate in your frog's tank to hide – make sure to clean out dead crickets on a regular basis.

**Worms**: Horned frogs are likely to eat a wide variety of worms. Juveniles should be fed small worms such as wax worms and small earthworms. As your frog grows you can begin adding other worms to the diet including mealworms, silk worms and large earthworms.

**Feeder Fish**: Giving your frog the occasional feeder fish is a great way to change up its diet. Keep in mind, however, that feeder fish have the potential to be carriers of disease – if the fish aren't healthy, they will pass their disease on to your frog. It is best to avoid feeder goldfish because they have a high fat content – rather, try guppies or other similar-sized tropical fish. To feed your frog fish, simply place them in its water bowl.

Chapter Five: Caring for Pac Man Frogs

**Pinkie Mice**: Pinkie mice are simply newborn mice – they are most often sold frozen. Before offering your frog a pinkie mouse, make sure to thaw it first and then place it in the tank using a pair of tongs. When your frog reaches its full size, you can even offer it small live mice.

**Supplements**: In order to prevent vitamin and mineral deficiency in your frogs, it is recommended that you dust feeder insects with a calcium and vitamin D3 powder. When using supplements, it is important not to overuse them – only dust your frog's food a once a week rather than at every feeding. Juvenile frogs, however, can receive supplements twice a week. If you raise your own feeder

## Chapter Five: Caring for Pac Man Frogs

insects, you should also be sure to provide them with healthy foods such as fresh fruits and vegetables so those nutrients can be transferred to your frog when it eats the insects.

### d.) Feeding Info Summary

**Diet**: carnivorous
**Nutritional Needs**: primary = protein, secondary = lipids, vitamins and minerals
**Vitamins and Minerals**: calcium, phosphorus, vitamin A, vitamin D3
**Feeding Juveniles**: daily; may also feed smaller amounts 3 times per week
**Feeding Adults**: once or twice per week
**Types of Food**: crickets, worms, feeder fish, pinkie mice
**Supplements**: powder; once per week for adults, twice per week for juveniles

Chapter Five: Caring for Pac Man Frogs

## 3.) Breeding Pac Man Frogs

*a.) Basic Breeding Info*

Breeding Pac Man Frogs can be quite a challenge, even for experienced amphibian owners. The reason for this is that horned frogs tend to be aggressive and very voracious eaters – they are just as likely to attack a potential mate as they are to breed with one. If you make an effort to recreate the natural environment of these frogs, however, you can encourage them to enter estivation (hibernation). After coming out of estivation, your frogs will be more likely to breed.

Chapter Five: Caring for Pac Man Frogs

## b.) The Breeding Process

The key to success in breedingPac Man Frogs is to encourage the frogs to go into estivation. Estivation is a sort of hibernation that horned frogs naturally go into when the temperature begins to drop. To induce estivation, slowly reduce the temperature in your frog's tank over a period of several days. Once your frog enters estivation, keep the temperature in the tank as stable as possible.

During estivation, your frog will neither eat nor drink but you must still provide fresh water on a daily basis to keep the cage damp. Your frog will bury itself into the substrate

## Chapter Five: Caring for Pac Man Frogs

and develop a casing of skin. This casing of skin will not be entirely shed but kept around the frog as a sort of cocoon. It is important that you do not disturb your frog while it is in this state – it will come out of estivation on its own once you begin to raise the tank temperature.

Estivation generally lasts about 2 months in the wild, so after two months you should begin gradually increasing the temperature in your frog tank until your frog awakens. Upon awakening, your frog will shed its skin casing and be ready to accept food. In addition to feeding, your frog should also be ready to breed.

To encourage breeding you will need to simulate the rainy season in your frog's natural habitat. To do so, place your breeding pair in the same terrarium and mist it frequently with fresh water. Observe your frogs during this time to make sure they do not hurt each other. Once mating has occurred you can remove the male frog from the tank. You may also want to add a few plants to the tank, if they are not there already, so the female has something to lay her eggs on.

Female horned frogs can lay between 1,000 and 2,000 eggs at a time. Once the eggs have been laid, remove the female or separate the eggs to prevent them from being eaten. After 2 to 3 days, the eggs should hatch and the tadpoles

## Chapter Five: Caring for Pac Man Frogs

will begin to develop. It is important to note that tadpoles are cannibalistic. If you do not want to raise all 1,000+ tadpoles to maturity, you can allow this cannibalism to occur naturally. Once the number of tadpoles has been pared down you can separate them into small cups and raise them individually.

### c.) Raising the Tadpoles

It generally takes between 3 and 5 weeks for metamorphosis to occur. Metamorphosis is the process through which tadpoles become juvenile frogs. When tadpoles first hatch, they have a long tail – over time they

## Chapter Five: Caring for Pac Man Frogs

develop legs. They also lose their round shape as their bones develop to give their bodies structure. Metamorphosis is an amazing process to witness – it is one of the joys of breedingPac Man Frogs.

If you decide to keep your tadpoles together in one tank, be sure to provide plenty of hiding places to reduce cannibalism. You should also feed your tadpoles small foods on a daily basis. The ideal foods for tadpoles include tubifex worms, black worms and chopped earthworms. Once the tadpoles have matured and the tail has been absorbed you can begin feeding them a traditional juvenile horned frog diet as described in the last section.

## Chapter Five: Caring for Pac Man Frogs

### d.) Breeding Info Summary:

**Breeding Preparations**: 2 months estivation (hibernation)
**Encouraging Breeding**: simulate rainy season
**Number of Eggs**: 1,000 to 2,000
**Hatching**: after 2 to 3 days
**Growth of Young**: metamorphosis from tadpoles into juvenile frogs
**Duration**: 3 to 5 weeks
**Food for Tadpoles**: black worms, tubifex worms, chopped earthworms
**Food for Juvenile Frogs**: small earthworms, wax worms
**Tips**: separate parents from eggs so they don't eat them; tadpoles may also be cannibalistic

# Chapter Five: Caring for Pac Man Frogs

## Chapter Six: Keeping Your Frogs Healthy

### 1.) Common Health Problems

Pac Man Frogs are a fairly healthy species in general but, like all animals, they are prone to developing disease at one point or another. Your best bet in raising a healthy frog is to make sure that the frog is healthy when you bring it home – if you buy a frog that is not in optimal condition, it is unlikely that its condition will improve under your care.

Frogs are very difficult to cure once they contract a disease. By familiarizing yourself with some of the most common horned frog health problems, however, you can diagnose

## Chapter Six: Keeping Your Frogs Healthy

diseases early and improve your frog's chances of making a recovery.

**Some of the common health problems seen in horned frogs include:**

- Metabolic Bone Disease
- Red Leg
- Water Edema Syndrome
- Toxic Out Syndrome
- Bacterial Infections
- Myasis
- Parasites
- Fungal Infections
- Blindness
- Impaction
- Nematode Infection
- Obesity

## Chapter Six: Keeping Your Frogs Healthy

### Metabolic Bone Disease

Also called MBD, metabolic bone disease is the result of a vitamin D3 or calcium deficiency. Due to this deficiency, the bones of the frog may become brittle and weak, making them more susceptible to breaks. Treatment and prevention of this disease involves supplementing the frog's diet with calcium and vitamin D3. These supplements come in the form of power which you can use to dust your frog's prey.

If you begin treatment in the early stages, you may be able to reverse the effects of the disease. Once metabolic bone disease reaches an advanced stage, however, it is generally not reversible. In extreme cases, you may be able to get an injectable calcium supplement from your veterinarian to help your frog recover from this disease.

**Causes**: vitamin D3 or calcium deficiency

**Symptoms**: bones of the frog may become brittle and weak

**Treatment**: supplementing the frog's diet with calcium and vitamin D3; injectable calcium supplement

## Chapter Six: Keeping Your Frogs Healthy

### Red Leg

This condition is fairly common in pet frogs but it can be somewhat difficult to diagnose. The main symptoms of red leg include lethargy and bloating – red spotting on the rear legs may also appear. Because Pac Man Frogs are naturally large and inactive, it is difficult to diagnose this disease early.

It may not be until the red spots appear that you are even aware your frog is sick. These spots are the result of burst blood vessels in the leg, caused by aeromonas bacteria. The only treatment for this condition is antibiotics. Even with treatment, however, the condition is often fatal.

**Causes**: aeromonas bacteria

**Symptoms:** lethargy and bloating – red spotting on the rear legs may also appear

**Treatment**: antibiotics

# Chapter Six: Keeping Your Frogs Healthy

## Water Edema Syndrome

This condition is caused by water retention which may result in the body of the frog swelling up. Water edema often follows some kind of heart or kidney disease.

There is no known treatment for this condition except for the possibility of making small incisions to drain the liquid, but this may not affect the outcome.

**Causes:** water retention; often a result of heart or kidney diseases

**Symptoms:** swelling in the body and legs

**Treatment:** no treatment known except for incisions to drain the liquid

## Chapter Six: Keeping Your Frogs Healthy

**Toxic Out Syndrome**

For horned frogs, the skin is an additional breathing organ – it can also absorb water to retain the frog's healthy moisture level. If you do not change the water in your frog's tank often enough, toxins can build up in the water which may then be absorbed through the frog's skin.

Some of the symptoms of this disease include erratic movements, spasms in the hind legs, lethargy and cloudy eyes. Treatment for this condition involves placing the frog in a dish of clean water, replacing the water every few hours until the symptoms disappear.

**Causes**: build-up of toxins in water, absorbed through the frog's skin

**Symptoms:** erratic movements, spasms in the hind legs, lethargy and cloudy eyes

**Treatment:** placing the frog in a dish of clean water, replacing the water every few hours

# Chapter Six: Keeping Your Frogs Healthy

## Bacterial Infections

It is not uncommon for horned frogs to be exposed to bacteria from time to time, but a healthy frog is generally able to fight off infection. If your frog's immune system is weakened due to injury or stress, however, he may not be able to fight off the infection.

A variety of factors may increase your frog's level of stress including foul water, improper lighting or temperature and physical injury. Some of the symptoms of bacterial infections include lack of appetite, lethargy, cloudy eyes, reddening of the skin and skin sloughing. Treatment for this condition may involve antibiotics or a tetracycline bath.

**Causes:** heightened stress due to foul water, improper lighting or temperature or physical injury

**Symptoms:** include lack of appetite, lethargy, cloudy eyes, reddening of the skin and skin sloughing

**Treatment:** antibiotics or a tetracycline bath

## Chapter Six: Keeping Your Frogs Healthy

**Myasis**

Myasis is a condition which arises when the frog is attacked by flies, maggots or other parasites. This condition is usually the result of an unclean environment, most likely dirty water. This disease is fairly easy to diagnose because you can generally see the flies and maggots swarming around the frog's head and body.

To treat this disease you may need to remove the maggots by hand with a pair of tweezers. After removing the maggots, clean the frog's cage thoroughly and sanitize it to prevent recurrence.

**Causes**: an unclean environment, most likely dirty water

**Symptoms:** flies and maggots swarming around the frog's head and body

**Treatment:** removal of maggots; cleaning and sanitizing the environment

# Chapter Six: Keeping Your Frogs Healthy

## Parasites

Horned frogs can be affected by a number of parasites including tapeworms, roundworms and pinworms. Though low levels of parasites are unlikely to harm your frog, you may want to have him checked out by a vet to be sure it won't turn into a problem.

Parasites are easily transferable so you should be especially careful if you keep two frogs in the same tank for breeding purposes. To be safe, you should quarantine the frogs first to make sure they do not carry parasites.

**Causes**: tapeworms, roundworms, pinworms, etc.

**Symptoms:** reddening of skin, skin becomes flaky

**Treatment:** veterinary diagnosis and treatment

## Chapter Six: Keeping Your Frogs Healthy

**Fungal Infections**

Pac Man Frogs are prone to developing several different kinds of fungal infections. These infections are particularly common in frogs that are subjected to high stress levels or unclean tanks. A fungal infection may appear in a variety of forms – in many cases it appears as cottony or wool-like white growths on the skin or mouth. Skin reddening may also be a symptom.

Fungal infections can generally be treated with antiseptics or fungicides. If the fungus enters the frog's blood stream, however, the infection becomes systemic and it may be much more difficult to treat. In order to achieve the best chance of recovery, you must reduce your frog's stress and clean the tank in addition to treating the infection.

**Causes**: high stress levels or unclean tanks

**Symptoms:** cottony or wool-like white growths on the skin or mouth; reddening of skin

**Treatment:** antiseptics or fungicides; reduce your frog's stress and clean the tank

## Chapter Six: Keeping Your Frogs Healthy

**Blindness**

Blindness in frogs is caused by lipid build-up in the corneas. This is a result of a diet that is too high in fat. If you feed your frog a diet that consists primarily of pinkie mice or other high-fat foods, your frog could be at risk for blindness. There is no cure for this condition but it can be prevented through feeding a healthy diet.

**Causes:** lipid build-up in the corneas; diet too high in fat

**Symptoms:** filming of the eyes, loss of sight

**Treatment:** no treatment; prevent with low-fat diet

## Chapter Six: Keeping Your Frogs Healthy

### Impaction

Impaction or intestinal obstruction is generally the result of the consumption of stones or gravel. As your frog feeds, he is likely to ingest small amounts of substrate. To prevent impaction, make sure the substrate in your frog's tank is soft – damp moss is best.

Symptoms you may notice in your frog include loss of appetite, decreased bowel movements and a hard lump in the belly. In some cases, the obstruction passes on its own – in severe cases, however, surgery may be the only option.

**Causes:** consumption of stones or gravel

**Symptoms:** loss of appetite, decreased bowel movements and a hard lump in the belly

**Treatment:** obstruction may pass on its own; extreme cases may require surgery

# Chapter Six: Keeping Your Frogs Healthy

## Nematode Infection

Nematodes are a type of roundworm – the most common genus affecting frogs is *Rhabdias*. The symptoms of this disease generally include rough or flaky skin, sloughing of the skin and graying or discoloration. Some frogs also exhibit rapid weight loss as a result of nematode infections.

Nematode infections can be very dangerous – particularly to frogs that are already stressed. This condition is, however, treatable as long as it is caught early. Treatment generally involves Thiabendazole or Ivermectin in the water dish.

**Causes:** nematodes, often of the genus *Rhabdias*

**Symptoms:** rough or flaky skin, sloughing of the skin and graying or discoloration

**Treatment:** Thiabendazole or Ivermectin in the water dish

## Chapter Six: Keeping Your Frogs Healthy

### Obesity

Pac Man Frogs are a fairly large species as it is, but if they become obese it can lead to serious health problems. Young frogs require a lot of food in order to grow properly but, if you do not taper off their diet once they mature, your frog is likely to become obese.

The result of obesity is generally a shortened lifespan. In severe cases, obesity can also cause other health problems such as digestive issues.

**Causes**: overfeeding, diet too high in fat

**Symptoms:** excess fat on the body

**Treatment:** reduce feeding, switch to foods with lower fat content

## Chapter Six: Keeping Your Frogs Healthy

### 2.) Preventing Illness

Because curing illness in Pac Man Frogs is very difficult, your best bet is to do whatever you can to prevent them in the first place. Follow these tips to help prevent your frogs from getting sick:

- Be very careful in buying horned frogs – take the time to select a specimen that appears healthy

- Do not buy a frog from a store that doesn't look clean or in which other animals appear to be sick

- Reduce your frog's stress level as much as possible by preventing any drastic changes in diet or environment

- Clean out your frog's water dish at least once a day and sanitize it regularly

- Offer your frog a healthy, varied diet to prevent nutritional deficiencies

- Make sure your frog's tank is properly ventilated – overly moist environments can foster fungal infections

## Chapter Six: Keeping Your Frogs Healthy

- Avoid exposing your frog to other frogs that have not been quarantined

- Do not handle your frog any more than necessary – the oils in your skin can harm your frog

- Make sure to buy your frog's food from a reputable source – contaminated food can wreak havoc on your frog's health.

- Use soft, moist substrate in your frog's tank rather than small stones or gravel

## Chapter Seven: Pac Man Frogs Care Sheet

### 1.) Basic Information

**Scientific Name**: *Ceratophrys ornate*
**Other Names**: Ornate Horned Frog, Pac Man Frog, Argentine Horned Frog
**Size**: up to 6 inches (15 cm)
**Weight**: up to 1 lbs. (480 g)
**Color**: green or yellowish green with black or red markings on the back
**Diet**: crickets, worms, feeder fish, snails, mice
**Lifespan**: 6 to 7 years average, up to 10 in captivity

## Chapter Seven: Pac Man Frogs Care Sheet

## 2.) Cage Set-up Summary

**Ideal Tank Size**: 10 gallons (38 liters)
**Cage Type**: glass aquarium/terrarium
**Tank Temperature**: 75° and 80° F (24° to 27° C)
**Tank Environment**: damp and humid
**Heating**: reptile heating pad affixed to underside of the tank
**Lighting**: fluorescent UVB bulb; red heat bulb in winter
**Substrate**: soft and damp; sphagnum or peat moss
**Water**: shallow dish, cleaned daily
**Other**: hiding places, live or artificial plants

## 3.) Feeding Info Summary

**Diet**: carnivorous
**Nutritional Needs**: primary = protein, secondary = lipids, vitamins and minerals
**Vitamins and Minerals**: calcium, phosphorus, vitamin A, vitamin D3
**Feeding Juveniles**: daily or 3 times per week
**Feeding Adults**: once or twice per week
**Types of Food**: crickets, worms, feeder fish, pinkie mice
**Supplements**: powder; once per week for adults, twice per week for juveniles

## Chapter Seven: Pac Man Frogs Care Sheet

### 4.) Breeding Info Summary

**Breeding Preparations**: 2 months estivation (hibernation)
**Encouraging Breeding**: simulate rainy season
**Number of Eggs**: 1,000 to 2,000
**Hatching**: after 2 to 3 days
**Growth of Young**: metamorphosis from tadpoles into juvenile frogs
**Duration**: 3 to 5 weeks
**Food for Tadpoles**: black worms, tubifex worms, chopped earthworms
**Food for Juvenile Frogs**: small earthworms, wax worms
Tips: separate parents from eggs so they don't eat them; tadpoles may also be cannibalistic

# Chapter Seven: Pac Man Frogs Care Sheet

## Chapter Eight: Common Mistakes Owners Make

**Housing Horned Frogs Together**

Though some species of frog can be, or even should be, kept in groups with their own species, this is not the case with Pac Man Frogs. Keeping two or more of these frogs together is likely to end in disaster – either one frog will attack the other or, if one frog is much smaller than the other, eat it outright. For the safety of your pet, do not keep more than one frog in the same cage and do not keep them with other pets.

## Chapter Eight: Common Mistakes Owners Make

**Overfeeding/Underfeeding**

Both overfeeding and underfeeding Pac Man Frogs can be very dangerous. If you do not feed these frogs properly in their youth, they may not grow correctly. Feeding mature frogs too much, however, can result in obesity which can lead to other health problems. Juvenile frogs can be fed small amounts of food (2 to 6 crickets) on a daily basis while adult frogs should only be fed two or three times a week. The larger the meal, the less often it should be given for adults.

**Feeding the Wrong Diet**

While the amount of food you offer your frog is very important, equally important is the type of food you give them. While many frog species are omnivorous or primarily insectivores, Pac Man Frogs are carnivorous. These frogs thrive on a diet of high-protein foods including insects, worms, small birds, fish, rodents and even other frogs. If you do not feed your frog a varied diet, it may suffer from nutritional deficiencies and might fail to thrive – it could also develop serious health problems.

# Chapter Eight: Common Mistakes Owners Make

## Improper Tank Setup

Pac Man Frogs are a terrestrial species which means that they spend more time on land than in the water. This is not to say, however, that they do not require water in their tank. Though a horned frog might not spend a great deal of time in the water itself, the water in the tank will help to keep the frog's environment warm and humid.

Another common mistake in regard to setting up a horned frog tank is the failure to include hiding places. These frogs spend a great deal of time burrowed into the substrate, lying in wait for prey to pass by. If you don't provide hiding places for your frog, it may become stressed and could fail to thrive.

# Chapter Eight: Common Mistakes Owners Make

**Failure to Follow Basic Safety Tips**

While Pac Man Frogs themselves are not dangerous, there are a few safety precautions you should take when keeping a pet frog. The following list provides a basic idea of recommended safety precautions:

- Always wash your hands with antibacterial soap after handing your frog or touching anything in the tank to prevent the spread of bacteria

- Keep the lid on your frog tank tightly sealed to prevent other pets from getting into the tank

- Avoid piling rocks or other tank décor items too high in your tank – your frog could injure itself in falling from these heights

- Make sure the water in your frog tank isn't so deep that your frog has trouble getting out – if necessary, line the bottom of the dish with stones

- When buying substrate for your frog tank, make sure it hasn't been treated with insecticides which could be harmful to your frog

## Chapter Eight: Common Mistakes Owners Make

- If you use gravel in your tank, be sure to wash it thoroughly in hot water before using it to remove dirt and other substances

- Always keep a spare UVB on hand and consider stocking an extra heating pad – in case one of yours breaks, you will not have to subject your frog to improper temperatures until you get a new one

# Chapter Eight: Common Mistakes Owners Make

## Chapter Nine: Frequently Asked Questions

### 1.) General Questions

**Q**: Why are Pac Man Frogs called Pac Man Frogs?

**A**: Horned frogs were given this name due to their resemblance to the video game character, Pac Man. Like Pac Man, these frogs have a round body and a very large mouth.

---

**Q**: Are Pac Man Frogs nocturnal or diurnal?

## Chapter Nine: Frequently Asked Questions

A: Most of these frogs are diurnal, though some are crepuscular (most active during the dawn and twilight hours). Like all frogs, horned frogs sleep with their eyes open.

---

Q: Can I keep two female horned frogs together?

A: Generally speaking, the females of any given species are typically less aggressive than the males. In regard to the Pac Man Frog, however, this is not necessarily true. Both sexes can be very aggressive and may try to attack or even eat another frog if kept in the same cage. This is why you must be very careful when keeping even a breeding pair together.

---

Q: Do Pac Man Frogs come in different colors?

A: The color of horned frogs varies depending on the species. Most Pac Man Frogs exhibit a base color of green or brown with red, orange, yellow or black markings. These frogs can also be found in albino form, having a yellow base color with orange markings.

---

Q: Why do these frogs have bumpy skin?

# Chapter Nine: Frequently Asked Questions

A: The bumps on the skin of horned frogs may look like warts, but they are not. This texture helps to break up the frog's shape when viewed from afar and also helps it to blend in to the leaf litter on the rainforest floor.

---

Q: Is a horned frog a good pet for a child?

A: The answer to this question varies depending on the individual child. Because these frogs are not meant to be handled, they may not be a good choice for a younger child or for a child that wants a pet that can be played with. If, however, your child is old enough to handle the responsibility of a frog, it may be a good choice. Before you buy your child a horned frog, make sure to inform him or her of the necessary responsibilities.

---

Q: If I don't want to keep my frog anymore, can I set it loose outside?

A: No, it is never a good idea to release non-native species like the horned frog into the wild. One reason is that your frog may not be able to survive on its own after being raised in captivity. Another reason, and perhaps a more important one, is that as a non-native species, horned frogs may

## Chapter Nine: Frequently Asked Questions

threaten local wildlife by competing for prey. If you absolutely cannot keep your frog anymore, take it to your local pet store or find another amphibian lover who will take it off your hands.

---

**Q:** Do Pac Man Frogs shed?

**A:** Yes, shedding is a natural part of a Pac Man Frog's life. When your frog is ready to shed, the outer layer of skin may lighten in color or become flaky. Do not be alarmed – it can take several hours or several days for a layer of skin to be completely shed so don't be tempted to "help" your frog by pulling at it.

## Chapter Nine: Frequently Asked Questions

### 2.) Questions about Feeding

**Q:** How can I add vitamins to my frog's diet?

**A:** Aside from using vitamin supplements, you can also gut load your feeder insects. Gut loading is simply the act of feeding insects healthy foods so the nutrients will be transferred to your frog when eaten. You can make your own gut loading formula using a mixture of poultry mash, tropical fish food, baby cereal and vegetables or fruits.

---

**Q:** Do I need to feed crickets once they are in my frog's tank?

**A:** Your frog may not eat all of the crickets you offer immediately after you put them in. If you want the crickets to stay alive until your frog gets around to catching them, you should provide them with both food and water. To give water to your crickets, simply soak a small sponge and place it in the tank. The crickets will be able to crawl on it and suck out the water they need.

---

**Q:** Can I feed my Pac Man Frog commercial amphibian pellets?

## Chapter Nine: Frequently Asked Questions

**A:** No, you shouldn't feed your frog commercial amphibian pellets. Not only is your frog unlikely to accept these pellets but they will not provide all of the nutrients your frog needs to be healthy. A healthy diet for horned frogs consists of a variety of different insects and small prey, supplemented with vitamins and minerals.

**Q:** What do I do if my frog won't eat?

**A:** If you have trouble getting your frog to eat when you first bring it home, it may be a matter of the kind of food you are offering. Pac Man Frogs are a carnivorous and predatory species – if you only offer them commercial frog pellets, they are unlikely to eat. These frogs require live prey and they like to have a variety of different foods in their diet. If your frog normally eats well but suddenly stops, it is more likely to be the result of a disease. Observe your frog for other signs of illness so you can identify the cause and seek treatment.

## Chapter Nine: Frequently Asked Questions

### 3.) Tank Setup and Maintenance Questions

**Q**: How do I clean my frog's tank?

**A**: Because the skin of horned frogs is sensitive and permeable, you need to be extremely careful about what products you use to clean their tanks. Never use any kind of chemical cleaning agent on the inside of your frog tank – even if you rinse it well, chemical residue could be left behind. If you must use soap inside the tank, use only mild dish detergent then rinse the tank several times and dry it completely. Food bowls and other items can be boiled in hot water to kill bacteria.

---

**Q**: Do I need to treat the water I use in my frog's tank?

**A**: Regular tap water is often treated with chlorine and other chemicals to make it safe for human consumption. These same chemicals may, however, be dangerous for frogs. The best solution is to use bottled spring water or drinking water in your frog tank. If you must use tap water, be sure to treat it with a dechlorinating solution first – these can be found in the aquarium aisle at your local pet store.

## Chapter Nine: Frequently Asked Questions

**Do not use distilled water because all of the minerals have been removed – minerals which are important for helping to maintain your frog's healthy bodily function.

---

**Q:** What is the ideal humidity level for my frog tank?

**A:** The best humidity level for a Pac Man Frog tank is between 50% and 70%. It is wise to install a simply hygrometer in your tank to make sure that the humidity level does not get too high or too low.

---

**Q:** Do I need to leaves the lights on in my frog tank for a certain period of time?

**A:** In order to help your frog maintain its natural biological rhythm, you should provide a proper day/night cycle. The longest amount of time you should leave your tank lights on is about 9 hours. To keep yourself from forgetting and leaving the lights on too long, purchase a basic automatic timer and set it to shut the lights off after 9 hours.

---

**Q:** How often do I need to replace the light bulb in my frog's tank?

# Chapter Nine: Frequently Asked Questions

**A**: Fluorescent bulbs typically last about 6 months. This may vary, however, depending how long you leave them on. Power compact fluorescent bulbs have a longer lifespan than traditional bulbs.

**Q**: Is it okay to keep a juvenile horned frog in a tank smaller than 10 gallons (38 liters)?

**A**: Technically, a juvenile frog can be kept in a tank smaller than 10 gallons (38 liters). This species is fairly inactive so, even when they are small, these frogs do not require a great deal of space. You will, however, need a larger tank once your frog reaches full size. To save yourself some money in the long run you may want to start out with a larger tank so you don't need to buy a replacement later.

**Q**: Why can't I use regular tap water in my frog tank?

**A**: City tap water is treated with chlorine and other chemicals in order to make it safe for human consumption. These same chemicals can be harmful to your frog, however, so they must be removed before you use the water in your frog's tank. Luckily, it is very easy to do so – all you have to do is treat the water with a few drops of de-chlorinating solution. You can find this solution in the

## Chapter Nine: Frequently Asked Questions

aquarium aisle at your local pet store. You can also purchase it online for less than $5 (£3.50).

## Chapter Nine: Frequently Asked Questions

### 4.) Horned Frog Care Questions

**Q**: Do albino horned frogs require any additional care?

**A**: The care of albino horned frogs is nearly identical to that of a traditional horned frog. The most important thing you need to be aware of is that albino frogs should not be exposed to UVB light. As an alternative, give your albino frog a little extra calcium supplement instead.

---

**Q**: If it becomes necessary, how can I safely handle my frog?

**A**: There are a number of reasons why you should avoid handling your horned frog whenever possible – the oils on your skin could harm your frog and your frog may be startled by the contact and could end up biting you. If you must handle your frog it is best to were powderless exam gloves. To pick up your frog, wrap your thumb and forefinger around the frog's waist, joining them at the tips under the frog's belly.

---

**Q**: What should I do if my frog bites me?

## Chapter Nine: Frequently Asked Questions

**A**: If you aren't careful in feeding your Pac Man Frog, it may mistake your finger for a bit of food and latch on. Because these frogs have sharp teeth, a bite can be very painful but you should try to resist the urge to shake your hand – doing so could send your frog flying across the cage. If you can wait for a few seconds, your frog is likely to let go. At this point you should immediately wash the bite in warm soapy water and apply an antibacterial ointment.

## Chapter Nine: Frequently Asked Questions

### 5.) Questions about Breeding

**Q:** How can I tell if my frog is pregnant?

**A:** The term "pregnant" is not usually applied to frogs because they spawn eggs – they do not give birth to live young. In many cases, a female frog will not look significantly different from normal when it is carrying eggs.

---

**Q:** How long after Pac Man Frog eggs are spawned will they hatch?

**A:** Hatching time may vary depending on the temperature in your frog's tank, but it generally happens 2 to 4 days after spawning. Remember, Pac Man Frogs tend to eat their own eggs and tadpoles so it is best to remove the adults from the tank as soon as the mating process has been completed.

---

**Q:** Do I have to separate the tadpoles after they hatch from their eggs?

**A:** It is your choice whether you separate the tadpoles or not. Tadpoles are cannibalistic so, if you want to raise most of your tadpoles to maturity you may want to either

## Chapter Nine: Frequently Asked Questions

provide hiding places or separate the tadpoles to minimize this cannibalism. Pac Man Frogs can lay 1,000 to 2,000 eggs at a time, however, so it may not be a bad thing to let nature run its course so you do not end up with too many adult frogs.

## Chapter Ten: Relevant Websites

1.) Food for Pac Man Frogs

**United States Websites:**

Millburn, Naomi. "The Feeding Habits of the Ornate Horned Frog." PawNation.
<http://animals.pawnation.com/feeding-habits-ornate-horned-frog-4076.html>

Kaplan, Melissa. "Ornate Horned Frogs." Herp Care Collection, Anapsid.org.
<http://www.anapsid.org/ornatacare.html>

## Chapter Ten: Relevant Websites

Edmonds, Devin. "Horned Frogs." Amphibian Care. <http://www.amphibiancare.com/frogs/caresheets/hornedfrog.html>

**United Kingdom Websites:**

"How to Care for Frogs and Toads." Exotic Pet Care. <http://www.exotic-pet-care>

"Horned Frog Care Sheet." The Amphibian.co.uk. <http://www.theamphibian.co.uk/Horned_frog_care>

Kells, Kelly. "Pets – Keeping Frogs and Toads." MookyChick. <http://www.mookychick.co.uk/how-to/how-to-guides/pets-frogs-and-toads.php>

## Chapter Ten: Relevant Websites

2.) Care for Pac Man Frogs

**United States Websites:**

"Ornate Horned Frog." LLL Reptile.
<http://lllreptile.com/info/library/animal-care>

"Ornate Horned Frog Caresheet." HerpCenter.com.
<http://www.herpcenter.com/reptile-caresheets/ornate-horned-frog.html>

"Ornate Horned Frog." Pet Supplies Plus.
<http://www.petsuppliesplusfl.com/AnimalCare/Reptiles/ornatehornedfrog.htm>

**United Kingdom Websites:**

"Disease." Dendroworld: FAQ.
<http://www.dendroworld.co.uk/FAQ/disease>

"Argentinean Horned Frog Care Sheet." Tyrannosaurus Pets. <http://www.tyrannosauruspets.co.uk/caresheets/46-care>

"Pac Man/Horned Frog Care." Reptile Expert.
<http://www.reptileexpert.org/Pac Man-frog-care>

## Chapter Ten: Relevant Websites

"Horned Frogs." AlphaPet Veterinary Clinics.
<http://alphapet.co.uk/pet-advice/reptiles/horned-frogs/>

## Chapter Ten: Relevant Websites

### 3.) Health Info for Pac Man Frogs

**United States Websites:**

"Choosing a Healthy Pet Frog." HubPages. <http://whitney05.hubpages.com/hub/healthy>

"Frog Health and Diseases." PopularPets.net. <http://www.popularpets.net/frogs/diseases.php>

"Common Illness in Pac Man Frogs." HubPages. <http://whitney05.hubpages.com/hub/pac-man-frog-health>

**United Kingdom Websites:**

"Amphibian Health and Disease. FrogLife. <http://www.froglife.org/disease>

"FAQs About Frogs: Health/Disease." WetWebMedia.com. <http://www.wetwebmedia.com/fwsubwebindex/GenFrogHlthF.htm>

"Prevention." All About Frogs. <http://allaboutfrogs.org/info/doctor/sick.html>

## Chapter Ten: Relevant Websites

### 4.) General Info for Pac Man Frogs

**United States Websites:**

"Argentine Horned Frog." The Animal Files.com. <http://www.theanimalfiles.com/amphibians/frogs/argentine_horned_frog.html>

"Horned Frog." A-Z Animals.com. <http://a-z-animals.com/animals/horned-frog/>

"South American Ornate Horned Frog." Animal Bytes. <http://www.seaworld.org/animal-info/animal-bytes/animalia/eumetazoa/coelomates/deuterostomes/chordates/craniata/amphibia/anura/south-american-ornate-horned-frog.htm>

**United Kingdom Websites:**

"Ornate Horned Frog." Dudley Zoological Gardens.<http://www.dudleyzoo.org.uk/our-animals/ornate-horned-frog>

"Ornate Horn Frog." The Living Rainforest. <http://www.the-livingrainforest.co.uk/living/view_caresheet.php?id=42>

## Chapter Ten: Relevant Websites

"Horned Frog Care Sheet." AnimalShop.co.uk.
<http://www.animalshop.co.uk/caresheets/amphibians/Frog_Horned.pdf.pdf>

# Index

## A

abnormal coloration ................................................................................. 36
aquarium .............................................................................. 7, 26, 40, 42, 43, 74
Argentina ............................................................................................. 4, 9, 16

## B

breed ............................................................................................. 22, 24, 39, 50, 52
breeders ......................................................................................................... 34
breeding ............................................................................. 2, 24, 27, 39, 51, 52, 54, 65
buying ................................................................................................. 2, 33, 34, 71

## C

cage ............................................................................................. 25, 31, 51, 64
calcium ...................................................................................... 30, 44, 48, 49, 59, 74
care ...................................................................................... 31, 37, 39, 57, 98, 99, 111, 112
carnivorous ........................................................................................... 44, 49, 74
cloudy eyes ............................................................................................... 62, 63
color ..................................................................................................... 1, 6, 16
common health problems ..................................................................................... 2, 58
costs ............................................................................................. 26, 27, 29, 30
Cranwell's horned frog ....................................................................................... 3
crickets ................................................................................. 1, 8, 46, 47, 49, 73, 74

## D

damaged skin .................................................................................................. 36
diet .................................................................... 1, 2, 32, 39, 44, 46, 47, 54, 59, 67, 70, 71
discharge ..................................................................................................... 37
disease ................................................................. 36, 45, 47, 57, 59, 61, 62, 64, 99, 101, 109

## E

| | |
|---|---|
| edema | 61 |
| eggs | 10, 52, 55, 75, 117 |
| endangered | 22, 23 |
| endangered species | 22 |
| estivation | 50, 51, 55, 75 |

## F

| | |
|---|---|
| feeder fish | 8, 29, 47, 49, 73, 74 |
| female | 6, 24, 52 |
| Fish and Wildlife Service | 22 |
| food | 4, 29, 31, 35, 37, 45, 47, 48, 52, 70, 72 |

## H

| | |
|---|---|
| habitat | 9, 12, 13, 14, 15, 17, 27, 35, 39, 52 |
| health problems | 45, 57, 70 |
| healthy | 1, 33, 37, 39, 44, 47, 49, 57, 62, 63, 67, 71, 101, 109 |
| healthy diet | 39, 44, 67 |
| heat | 40, 42, 43, 74 |
| heater | 27 |
| heating pad | 42, 43, 74 |
| hibernation | 50, 51, 55, 75 |
| hide | 27, 42, 47 |
| household pets | 25 |
| humid | 40, 43, 74 |

## I

| | |
|---|---|
| Impaction | 58, 68 |
| infection | 63 |
| initial costs | 26 |
| intestinal obstruction | 68 |

## J

| | |
|---|---|
| juvenile | 40, 46, 53, 54, 55, 75 |

## L

| | |
|---|---|
| lethargy | 62, 63 |
| license | 21, 22, 32 |
| licensing regulations | 21 |
| lifespan | 4, 70 |
| lighting | 26, 28, 31, 42, 63 |
| local council | 22, 23 |

## M

| | |
|---|---|
| male | 6, 24, 52 |
| metabolic bone disease | 59 |
| metamorphosis | 53, 55, 75 |
| monthly costs | 26 |
| Myasis | 58, 64 |

## N

| | |
|---|---|
| noise | 32 |
| nutritional deficiencies | 71 |
| nutritional needs | 44 |

## O

| | |
|---|---|
| obesity | 44, 45, 70 |
| ornate horned frog | 3, 4 |

## P

| | |
|---|---|
| parasites | 64, 65 |
| permit | 21, 22, 23, 32 |

pet store ..........................................................................26, 27, 34, 40, 41, 47
pinkie mice..................................................................1, 29, 46, 49, 67, 74
prevention ............................................................................................ 59
pros and cons........................................................................................ 31
protein ...................................................................................... 44, 49, 74
purchase ................................................... 10, 21, 26, 27, 28, 31, 33, 40, 42
purchasing .............................................................................. 23, 33, 35

# R

regulations ............................................................................................ 22

# S

space .................................................................................................... 31
species ............. 3, 9, 10, 11, 12, 13, 14, 15, 16, 17, 18, 22, 32, 36, 37, 39, 40, 57, 70, 109
sphagnum moss .................................................................................... 27
state laws ............................................................................................. 22
substrate .....................................................4, 7, 26, 27, 29, 30, 32, 40, 42, 47, 51, 68, 72
supplements ..........................................................................29, 47, 48, 59
symptoms ........................................................................................ 62, 63

# T

tadpoles ..........................................................................52, 53, 54, 55, 75
tank ...........1, 2, 7, 26, 27, 28, 30, 40, 41, 42, 43, 47, 48, 51, 52, 54, 62, 65, 68, 71, 72, 74
tank thermometer ................................................................................ 30
teeth ................................................................................................... 5, 7
temperature ........................................................... 7, 27, 41, 42, 51, 52, 63
terrarium ....................................................................... 7, 40, 43, 52, 74
toxins ................................................................................................... 62
treatment.............................................................................59, 61, 65, 67

# U

UVB lamp ............................................................................................. 28

## V

vitamin D3 ................................................................ 30, 45, 48, 49, 59, 74
vitamins and minerals ............................................................... 30, 44, 49, 74

## W

water ........................................... 7, 27, 28, 40, 42, 47, 51, 52, 61, 62, 63, 64, 71
water dish ............................................................................... 27, 28, 42, 71
worms .................................................... 1, 7, 8, 29, 47, 49, 54, 55, 73, 74, 75

# References

"Amphibian Health and Disease. FrogLife. <http://www.froglife.org/disease>

"Argentine Horned Frog." The Animal Files.com. <http://www.theanimalfiles.com/amphibians/frogs/argentine_horned_frog.html>

Browne, Robert K. "Amphibian Diet and Nutrition." AArk Science and Research. <https://aark.portal.isis.org/researchguide/amphibian%20husbandry/amphibian%20diet%20and%20nutrition.pdf>

"Ceratophrys ornata," AmphibiaWeb. <http://amphibiaweb.org/cgi/amphib_query?where-genus=Ceratophrys&where-species>

"Ceratophrys ornata," IUCN Red List. <http://www.iucnredlist.org/details/56340/0>

"Choosing a Healthy Pet Frog." HubPages. <http://whitney05.hubpages.com/hub/healthy>

"Common Illness in Pac Man Frogs." HubPages. <http://whitney05.hubpages.com/hub/pac-man-frog-health>

Edmonds, Devin. "Horned Frogs." Amphibian Care. <http://www.amphibiancare.com/frogs/caresheets/hornedfrog.html>

"FAQs About Frogs: Health/Disease." WetWebMedia.com. <http://www.wetwebmedia.com/fwsubwebindex/GenFrogHlthF.htm>

"Frequently Asked Questions About Frogs." Drs. Foster and Smith. <http://www.drsfostersmith.com/pic/article.cfm?aid=2616>

"Frequently Asked Questions About Frogs and Toads." University of Florida Wildlife Extension. <http://www.wec.ufl.edu/extension/wildlife_info/faq/frogstoads.php>

"Frog Health and Diseases." PopularPets.net. <http://www.popularpets.net/frogs/diseases.php>

"Frog Safety 101." Dendroboard.com. <http://www.dendroboard.com/forum/care-sheets/25053-frog-safety-101-a.html>

"Horned Frog." A-Z Animals.com. <http://a-z-animals.com/animals/horned-frog/>

"Horned Frog Care Sheet." The Amphibian.co.uk.
<http://www.theamphibian.co.uk/Horned_frog_care>

"Horned (Pac-Man) Frog." J and K's Pet Depot.
<http://www.jandkspetdepot.com/wp-content/uploads/2011/06/Horned-Pac-Man-Frog.pdf>

"How Much Does a Pet Frog Cost?" CostHelper.com.
<http://pets.costhelper.com/frog.html>

Kaplan, Melissa. "Ornate Horned Frogs." Herp Care Collection, Anapsid.org.
<http://www.anapsid.org/ornatacare.html>

Millburn, Naomi. "The Feeding Habits of the Ornate Horned Frog." PawNation.
<http://animals.pawnation.com/feeding-habits-ornate-horned-frog-4076.html>

"Ornate Horn Frog." The Living Rainforest.
<http://www.the-livingrainforest.co.uk/living/view_caresheet.php?id=42>

"Ornate Horned Frog." LLL Reptile.
<http://lllreptile.com/info/library/animal-care>

"Ornate Horned Frog." Dudley Zoological Gardens.<http://www.dudleyzoo.org.uk/our-animals/ornate-horned-frog>

"Pac Man/Horned Frog Care." Reptile Expert. <http://www.reptileexpert.org/Pac Man-frog-care>

"Pac Man Frog." Heathwood.org. <http://www.heathwood.org/simpson/quicklinks/animalsoftherainforest/Pac Man.htm>

"Pac Man Frog." ZooMed.org. <http://zoomed.com/cm/resources-stuff/Care%20Sheet/fb_Pac ManFrog.html>

"Pac Man Frog/Ornate Horned Frog." Pet Supplies Plus. <http://www.petsuppliesplus.com/content.jsp?pageName=pac_man_frog>

"Pac Man Frog Care Guide." Reptiles-N-Critters.com. <http://www.reptilesncritters.com/care-guide-Pac Man-frog.php>

"Some Common Questions: Concerning Keeping Frogs and Toads as Pets." AllAboutFrogs.org. <http://allaboutfrogs.org/info/doctor/common.html#pregnant>

"South American Ornate Horned Frog." Animal Bytes. <http://www.seaworld.org/animal-info/animal-

bytes/animalia/eumetazoa/coelomates/deuterostomes/chordates/craniata/amphibia/anura/south-american-ornate-horned-frog.htm>

Team, Ben. "Different Ways to Set Up Pac Man Frog Cages." PawNation. <http://animals.pawnation.com/different-ways-set-up-Pac Man-frog-cages-5758.html>

# Photo Credits

Title Page, By Flickr.com user "avmaier" (http://www.flickr.com/photos/kookyworld/179786266/) [CC-BY-2.0 (http://creativecommons.org/licenses/by/2.0)], via Wikimedia Commons

Page 1 Photo, By Flickr user Dwmizell, <http://www.flickr.com/photos/dwmizell/5402010573/sizes/l/in/photostream/>

Page 3 Photo, By Pierre-Yves Vaucher (http://www.batraciens-reptiles.com) (http://calphotos.berkeley.edu) [CC-BY-SA-2.5 (http://creativecommons.org/licenses/by-sa/2.5) or CC-BY-SA-2.5 (http://creativecommons.org/licenses/by-sa/2.5)], via Wikimedia Commons

Page 6 Photo, By OpenCage.info, <http://opencage.info/pics.e/large_7250.asp>

Page 12 Photo, By Flickr user Mike Baird, <http://www.flickr.com/photos/mikebaird/5008409819/>

Page 13 Photo, By Mauricio Rivera Correa (http://calphotos.berkeley.edu) [CC-BY-SA-2.5 (http://creativecommons.org/licenses/by-sa/2.5) or CC-BY-

SA-2.5 (http://creativecommons.org/licenses/by-sa/2.5)], via Wikimedia Commons

Page 14 Photo, By Flickr user Maarten Sepp, <http://www.flickr.com/photos/9616707@N07/2060606462/sizes/z/in/photostream/>

Page 15 Photo, By Flickr user Fbiole, <http://commons.wikimedia.org/wiki/File:Cranwell's_horned_frog.jpg>

Page 16 Photo, By Grosscha (Own work) [GFDL (http://www.gnu.org/copyleft/fdl.html) or CC-BY-SA-3.0 (http://creativecommons.org/licenses/by-sa/3.0)], via Wikimedia Commons

Page 17 Photo, By Slick-Bot, via Wikimedia Commons, <http://en.m.wikipedia.org/wiki/File:Ceratophrys_cornuta_01.jpg>

Page 18 Photo, By Flickr user Jeffledoux, <http://www.flickr.com/photos/jeffledoux/7983766950/sizes/z/in/photostream/>

Page 21 Photo, By Flickr user DanCentury, <http://www.flickr.com/photos/dancentury/125936480/sizes/l/in/photostream/>

Page 24 Photo, By Flickr user Rusty Clark, <http://www.flickr.com/photos/rusty_clark/6315952681/sizes/l/in/photostream/>

Page 25 Photo, By Flickr user Me and the Sysop, <http://www.flickr.com/photos/pyxopotamus/4600745184/sizes/z/in/photostream/>

Page 34 Photo, By Flickr user DanCentury, <http://www.flickr.com/photos/grumpychris/57735652/sizes/l/in/photostream/>

Page 37 Photo, By Flickr user Mike Baird, <http://www.flickr.com/photos/mikebaird/5009018830/sizes/l/in/photostream/>

Page 39 Photo, By Mike Baird [CC-BY-2.0 (http://creativecommons.org/licenses/by/2.0)], via Wikimedia Commons

Page 41 Photo, By Flickr user Ecov Ottos, <http://www.flickr.com/photos/ottosv/4113520915/sizes/l/in/photostream/>

Page 45 Photo, By Flickr user DanCentury, <http://www.flickr.com/photos/dancentury/145815335/sizes/z/in/photostream/>

Page 46 Photo, By LEAPTOUY (Own work) [Public domain], via Wikimedia Commons, <http://commons.wikimedia.org/wiki/File:Bolikhamxay_Thabok_Crickets.JPG>

Page 48 Photo, By Perhols, via Wikimedia Commons, <http://th.m.wikipedia.org/wiki/%E0%B9%84%E0%B8%9F%E0%B8%A5%E0%B9%8C:Guppy_pho_0048.jpg>

Page 50 Photo, By OpenCage.info, <http://opencage.info/pics/large_14520.asp>

Page 51 Photo, By Flickr user Aranya Sen, <http://www.flickr.com/photos/aranyasen/1558676713/sizes/z/in/photostream/>

Page 53 Photo, By Flickr user Zach Welty, <http://www.flickr.com/photos/zwww/6134529171/sizes/l/in/photostream/>

Page 54 Photo, By Palosirkka, via Wikimedia Commons, <http://commons.wikimedia.org/wiki/File:Frog_eggs>

Page 56 Photo, By Maarten Sepp (Own work) [GFDL (http://www.gnu.org/copyleft/fdl.html) or CC-BY-SA-3.0-2.5-2.0-1.0 (http://creativecommons.org/licenses/by-sa/3.0)], via Wikimedia Commons

Page 72 Photo, By OpenCage.info, <http://opencage.info/pics.e/large_1540.asp>

Page 75 Photo, By Flickr user DanCentury, <http://www.flickr.com/photos/dancentury/125940637/sizes/l/in/photostream/>

Page 80 Photo, By Andreas Schlüter [CC-BY-SA-2.5 (http://creativecommons.org/licenses/by-sa/2.5) or CC-BY-SA-2.5 (http://creativecommons.org/licenses/by-sa/2.5)], via Wikimedia Commons

Page 94 Photo, By Max (Own work) [GFDL (http://www.gnu.org/copyleft/fdl.html) or CC-BY-SA-3.0-2.5-2.0-1.0 (http://creativecommons.org/licenses/by-sa/3.0)], via Wikimedia Commons

www.ingramcontent.com/pod-product-compliance
Lightning Source LLC
LaVergne TN
LVHW021120080426
835510LV00012B/1764